WHERE LOVING MEMORIES GRACED

by
Naomi Argo Warren

Compiled by
Heather M. Glenn

I hope you enjoy this book. Naomi, the author, is my grandmother. I rejoice that I will get to see her again in heaven!! :)

Where Loving Memories Graced
by Naomi Argo Warren

Printed in the United States of America

ISBN 1-594672-23-7

Xulon Press
www.XulonPress.com

Xulon Press books are available in bookstores everywhere, and on the Web at www.XulonPress.com.

Amanda,

I am so proud of you. It just seems like yesterday that you were sitting in my third grade class. Where does time go? I am very proud of the young woman that you have become. Your love for the Lord shows in your face. He has blessed me to be able to watch you grow up. You have always had a special place in my heart. Best Wishes to you as you continue your journey in life. God Bless You!! Love in Christ

Jaton McGraw

This book is dedicated to the memory of Naomi Argo Warren.
We love and miss you dearly.

Table of Contents

TO

KNOW

GOD

CREATION

In the beginning God created the earth,
That's the way the Bible begins;
The earth was void, without form,
And in darkness from end to end;
His spirit moved upon the waters deep,
His creation He began to complete.

But first, He said, we must have light,
Then He said that it was good,
The light, He decided to call it day,
The darkness, He would call night,
If we combine them both together, said He,
Evening and morning the first day shall be.

Let there be a firmament in the midst
Of waters, let it be so divided,
The waters below from the waters above,
In an atmosphere of space, He decided,
The firmament shall be called Heaven, said He,
Evening and morning the second day shall be.

Let the waters under the heavens be gathered, as planned,
Into one place let them be,
This gathering of waters shall be called seas,
The remaining will be called earth land
With grass and herb yielding seed, said He,
Evening and morning the third day shall be.

We need lights in the firmament of Heaven,
In fact, we need two for sight,
A greater light to rule the day,
And a lesser one for the night;
We shall make myriads of stars, said He,
Evening and morning the fourth day shall be.

We need creatures to move in the water break,
To abundantly bring forth their kind,
Great whales and fowl to fly in the air,
All living creatures that moveth, we'll make;
They shall be blessed, fruitful and multiplied, said He,
Evening and morning the fifth day shall be.

Let us make man in our own image,
Male and female we shall create,
To rule over every living thing under Heaven, said He,
Evening and morning the sixth day shall be;
So God created the heavens and earth,
And rested from His work on day seven.

And the Lord God formed man of the dust of the ground, and breathed into his nostrils the breath of life, and man became a living soul. (Gen. 2:7 KJV)

GOD SEES

God sees you when you're happy
And rejoices at your mirth;
He sees your deep depression
And reassures your worth.
God sees your pain and suffering
And feels your hurt inside,
And when He sees your anger,
He calms your passioned pride.
God sees you when you're sinning
And draws you close to Him,
Forgives you and accepts you
As a child, does not condemn.

Behold, the eye of the Lord is upon them that fear him, upon them that hope in his mercy; (Ps. 33:18 KJV)

TO KNOW GOD

The beauty of thy world,
With loving hands unfurled,
With majesty and splendor,
With open arms so tender;
Sublime in all its glory,
Reveal to us the story
Of God's redemptive plan,
To save the soul of man.

In righteousness and mercy,
Words uttered so conversely,
To bridge the link dividing,
Between our spirits abiding;
Your sovereign will to give,
Abundant life to live,
Thy being so magnificent,
Omnipresent, omniscient, omnipotent.

The heavens declare the glory of God; and the firmament sheweth his handiwork. (Ps. 19:1 KJV)

POETIC PROVERBS

Don’t fail to correct your children,
For they need it once in a while,
Discipline won't hurt them,
And you'll have a much better child.

Don't waste your breath on a rebel,
For it will all be in vain,
He will despise the wisest advice,
And refuse it again and again.

Do not rob the poor and the sick,
And think that you will prosper,
For the Lord is their defender,
Their miseries not to foster.

A cheerful heart does good like a medicine,
And does not taste nearly as badly,
But a broken spirit makes one sick,
Leaves you feeling unhappy and sadly.

A rebel doesn't care about the facts,
Nor of the times or seasons,
All he wants to do is yell,
Tune out the voice of reason.

A fool gets into constant fights,
Sometimes ends up in suing,
If only he had known that
His mouth is his undoing.

What dainty morsels rumors are,
We devour with avid sensation,
They are eaten with great relish,
To nourish our temptations.

Pride ends in destruction,
And overcomes your soul,
Humility ends in honor,
Is worthy of your goal.

Hard work means prosperity,
Not for a ladder to climb,
Busily filling each moment for
Only a fool idles away his time.

Work hard and become a leader,
A message that we heed,
'Tis better to strive and lose than
Be lazy and never succeed.

Don't tell your secrets to a gossip,
And expect them not unfurled,
Don't give them your innermost feelings,
Unless you want them broadcast to the world.

The wicked will finally lose,
In the end all is lost,
The righteous will finally win,
Be willing to pay the cost.

The Lord preserves the upright,
His righteousness to behold,
He ruins the plans of the wicked,
But beckons him come to the fold.

Pride goes before destruction,
Haughtiness before a fall,
We must be watchful and guarded,
It can happen to us all.

It is better to eat soup with someone you love,
Than steak with someone you hate,
'Tis better to trust in Jesus' death,
Than leave it all to fate.

Wise men are praised for their wisdom,
Are cherished and ardently sought,
Fools are despised for their folly,
And try to be noticed for naught.

The good man eats to live,
To nourish his body to health,
While the evil man lives to eat,
Sometimes cannot enjoy his wealth.

Hard work brings prosperity,
To labor is fine and good,
Playing around brings poverty,
Must not be misunderstood.

Self control means controlling the tongue,
The hardest thing to do,
A quick retort can ruin everything,
Too late to rescue you.

To hate is to be a liar,
To slander is to be a fool,
So don't use your tongue for evil,
And let Satan have a tool.

Just as Death and Destruction are never satisfied, so human desire is never satisfied. (Prov. 27:20 NLT)

A LETTER TO THE RADIO TEACHER
(FROM A FOREIGN BROADCAST)

Dear Sir

Is there really a Jesus Christ?
I'm curious, but I have doubt,
Who is he, where did he come from,
How can I find him out?
Who is his mother, who is his father?
What is Christianity all about?
I've never heard of your Christ before,
Please, Sir, could you tell me a little bit more?

You see, Sir, where I come from,
It's all so strange to me,
Our Holy Book does not speak of Christ,
Or how he came to be;
But since I got my radio,
I listen to you daily,
I set my alarm to awaken me,
Every morning at half past three.

I'm interested in what you say,
And desire to study with you,
Is it possible to get a copy of your Bible
So I can read it too?
Would this Jesus of yours save me,
Would you tell me what I must do?
If I could be changed from old to new,
I'd like to know your Jesus too.

Your teaching is very important,
As it comes in clear through the air,
But why don't you speak an hour or more,
An half hour is not long to share;

I've noticed changes in my nature,
Your words give me peace there,
I hope this book of yours is free,
For I have no money to send, you see.

You may not know, but in my country,
It's so hard to believe what you say,
For if you change your religion here,
You'll be persecuted every day,
For they don't know about your Christ
And this forgiving spirit way,
But he seems to be a very good man,
I'd like to know more about him, if I can.

I sure do like to listen
And I hope you don't mind what I say,
But if Jesus is still alive,
Where is his dwelling today?
Will Jesus ever come back again,
Do you think he will come my way?
Sir, if you could send me a bible,
I promise to read it each day.

Your friend,

P.S. Please send it without delay.

For everyone who asks, receives. Everyone who seeks, finds.
And the door is opened to everyone who knocks.
(Luke 11:10 NLT)

IF I COULD

If I could see what God sees,
I'd have all seeing eyes;
If I could hear what God hears,
I'd hear no sad goodbyes.

If I could smell as God smells,
Sweet odors I'd enjoy;
If I could feel as God feels,
No sorrows would annoy.

If I knew what God knew,
I wonder if my mirth,
Would change in fear of
What's coming on the earth.

O Lord, how great are thy works! and thy thoughts are very deep. (Ps. 92:5 KJV)

I DON'T BELIEVE

I don't believe in greed,
Yet selfish desires I feed.

I don't believe in lying,
Yet untruths keep I sighing.

I don't believe in pride,
Yet conceit I try to hide.

I don't believe in vanity,
Yet indulge it with insanity.

I don't believe in anger,
Yet passions of rage endanger.

I don't believe in unkind,
Yet do it all the time.

I don't believe in covet,
Yet cannot rise above it.

I don't believe in carrying,
All of these sins a glaring.

Only one thing left to do,
Let Jesus walk in my shoe.

Commit thy way unto the Lord; trust also in him; and he shall bring it to pass. (Ps. 37:5 KJV)

VANITY (ECCLESIASTES)

The words of the preacher say to us,
Vanity of vanities, all is vanity;
When our labor is only for profit,
What good does it do humanity?

Generations come and go, he says,
The sun rises and runs to and fro,
The winds blow north and south,
But nowhere do they go.

The rivers busily run into the sea,
And yet they are never full,
The waters return to the rivers,
Back and forth like a magnet pull.

History merely repeats itself,
Nothing is really new,
We know it's all been done before,
So really, what can you point to?

So I gave my heart to search out wisdom,
Concerning all things under the sun;
That which is crooked cannot be made straight,
A vexation of spirit, I've won.

I found in my search for understanding,
The lot of man is like chasing the wind,
What is wrong cannot be righted,
No use thinking what might have been.

I worked hard to get wisdom,
The more my wisdom, the more my grief,
I found that I was chasing the wind,
With more wisdom, my distress, no relief.

Come now, be merry, I told myself,
I decided to try the road of drink,
Still seeking for my wisdom though,
It too was vanity, I did think.

Then I changed to the life of folly,
So I could experience my ultimate goal
Of complete happiness in my life,
I found it too was vanity out of control.

I then turned to material things,
Homes, vineyards, parks, and gardens I sought,
I had herds, flocks, silver, and gold,
Anything my eyes wanted, I bought.

One day I look upon all my labors,
And one conclusion I came by,
The wise and foolish have one thing in common,
Just as a fool dies, so will I.

So what good is wisdom,
For both the wise and foolish die,
We will both be soon forgotten,
When in the grave we lie.

I decided it was foolish indeed
To leave the fruits of my work for tomorrow,
To those who have never worked before,
To inherit my labor without charge or sorrow.

There is a right time for everything,
A time to be born, a time to die,
A time to plant, a time to harvest,
A time to laugh and a time to cry.

There's a time to be quiet, a time to speak up,
A time for war, a time for peace,
A time for loving, a time for hating,
A time to tear and repair, a time to cease.

Whatever God does is final,
Nothing can be added or taken away,
We should enjoy the fruits or our labor,
That God so graciously provides today.

He who loves money never has enough,
The more you have, the more you spend,
So enjoy your work, accept your fate,
It's a gift of God, your joy to send.

The day one dies is better than
The day that one is born,
The wise man thinks much of death,
The foolish, a good time from night to morn.

Enjoy prosperity whenever you can,
But when hard times strike and you're hurtin',
Remember, God gives one as well as the other,
For nothing in this life is certain.

So keep on sowing seed every day,
You'll never know which ones will grow,
Enjoy the fruits of your labor, but remember,
We give account to God what we sow.

Honor God in your youth before evil days come,
When the silver lining left in your clouds fade,
When the dust returns to the earth as it was,
The spirit returns to the God who gave.

My final conclusion after all my study:
Fear God, obey His commandments true,
For this is the entire duty of man,
For God will judge what we say and do.

Remember now thy Creator in the days of thy youth, while the evil days come not, nor the years draw nigh, when thou shalt say, I have no pleasure in them; (Eccl. 12:1 KJV)

EARTHLY ANGELS

The closest thing to angelic beings,
God allowed us here on earth,
Is the dimpled cheek of a baby's smile,
Full of piety and mirth;
Two twinkling eyes so full of trust,
Pure and innocent giving,
The kind of love to melt the heart
Of the vilest human living.

I will praise thee; for I am fearfully and wonderfully made: marvellous are thy works; and that my soul knoweth right well. (Ps. 139:14 KJV)

IF I COULD CHANGE THE WORLD

If I could change the world
And have my plans unfurled,
I wonder what I'd do
To see them carried through,
Would I be just and wise
Like Solomon to advise.
Could I see inside the mind,
Be content with what I'd find;
With all that power so great,
I surely would not hesitate
To feed the hungry, clothe the poor,
Provide good jobs for every doer;
And if I could, I'd heal the sick,
I'd do it fast and very quick;
Everyone could see and hear,
No more sorrows, not one little tear,
All wars would cease
And there'd be peace,
If I could change the world.

If I could change the world,
Like magic to be hurled,
I'd provide all your worldly needs,
With kindness and compassionate deeds;
I'd gladly give you joy and health,
A happy home with lots of wealth;
Yes, I could give you all of this,
But the greatest thing, you still could miss,
For there's one thing I could never do,
And that's to save your soul for you;
Though I provide for everything,
Salvation I could never bring,
Happiness I could never give,
For that's an inner thing you live;

Whatever I could do
To make a change in you,
I'd still unhappy be,
Without a change inside of me.

First, help me never to tell a lie. Second, give me neither poverty nor riches! Give me just enough to satisfy my needs. For if I grow rich, I may deny you and say, "Who is the Lord?" And if I am too poor, I may steal and thus insult God's holy name. (Prov. 30:8,9 NLT)

O WINTRY WIND

O wintry wind, O mighty wintry wind,
I yearn to know you and comprehend,
Why cometh in with such a scowl,
Always so angry and on the prowl;
Your bitter sting makes red my face,
Where goeth thou in such a hurried pace,
O mighty wintry wind.

I bundle up from head to toe,
And try to be your friend, you know,
But still you bring my eyes to tears,
You nip my nose, laugh at my fears;
I know some people welcome you,
But I must say, I rarely do,
O wintry, wintry wind.

But when you're calm and all is still,
My heart is warmed with how I feel,
For I am snug and safe inside,
With food and warmth God has supplied,
Then I can bow my head and say,
I thank you God for a winter day,
And the mighty wintry wind.

The wind goeth toward the south, and turneth about unto the north; it whirleth about continually, and the wind returneth again according to his circuits. (Eccl. 1:6 KJV)

MEDITATION

When we in silent meditation
Bemused and introspective,
Our minds in random to and fro,
Old memories resurrected;
At times not wanting to look back,
Unhappy thoughts to ponder,
Our hearts do fill with sadness,
Our souls to tear asunder.

For sins past, we've asked you for
Forgiveness and regeneration,
We know without doubt, your word
Has promised us restoration;
At other times when Satan comes
To make our guilt more heavy,
We open wide our hearts to him,
Bid him enter, our souls to levy.

He fills us with doubts and shame
Of memories brought to surface,
And if we let him linger there,
To depths below, he'll hurl us;
He weighs us down with burdens great,
Our struggles all so weary,
He prods us on to failure,
Our life to be so dreary.

You said that you'd remove our sins
As far as east is from the west,
That you would remember them no more,
To bury with all the rest,

And so we thank you dear Lord
That we can meditate and pray,
And know within our hearts,
You'll hear everything we say.

We bless your name above all else,
And praise you for your favor,
Without your love and mercy, Lord,
We'd be without a Savior;
You fill us with your presence,
Our souls in worship be,
You calm our fears, increase our faith,
Dear God in Heaven, we thank thee.

Give ear to my words, O Lord, consider my meditation.
(Ps. 5:1 KJV)

HOW CAN YOU?

How can you know a loss, and never had a gain,
How can you feel the ease, yet never had no pain.

How can you be asleep, yet dream as though awake,
How can you know what's real, and never known a fake.

How can you know what's sour, and never tasted sweet,
How can you feel the cool, if you've never borne the heat.

How can you be sad, and never, never glad,
How can you know what's good unless you know what's bad.

How can you wear a frown and never wear a smile,
How can you be a grownup and never been a child.

Unless you've been in bondage, how can you be free,
And if you never were, how can you really be.

If you've never tried, how can you know to fail,
How can you believe in Heaven and not believe in Hell.

How can you be saved unless you know you've sinned,
How can you have a beginning and never have an end.

How can you go on sinning and claim that all is well,
How can you reject the Savior and send your soul to hell.

Wisdom is the principal thing; therefore get wisdom: and with all thy getting get understanding. (Prov. 4:7 KJV)

GOD'S RAIN

How does God show his love to us,
Many ways in nature giving;
Just the simple things we see each day,
All for our pleasure in living.

When the rain beats down upon our roof,
Sometimes in torrents raging,
It's only the Lord our God depicting
A drama for us he's staging.

When the lightnings, thunders, and storms come near,
Our spirits to try and grieve,
It's only God with his almighty power,
Beckoning and calling you to believe.

When the gentle, little drops of rain
Hit the ground softly, then fall apart,
It's only the Lord whispering to you,
Soothing and calming your troubled heart.

It is I, the Lord is saying to you,
Awake, do away with your sorrows,
For I have given you one day more,
I have not promised tomorrows.

After a shower in springtime comes,
And the sunshine peeps through the cloud,
It seems as though all nature wakes up,
And nods, and thanks the Lord, so proud.

The little flowers, so young and fresh,
Just beginning to grow and live,
Perk up their little ears and say,
Thank you God for the showers you give.

The little birds start singing out,
Hidden in silence while the rains came,
The leaves on the trees are nodding about,
Renewing once more, new life to gain.

All is well, washed and cleansed,
All nature winks with glee,
Happiness overflows and runs
Like a river into the sea.

God has shown his majesty great,
Once more to nature and all mankind,
He's freely given the rain to us,
To nourish, cleanse, and renew our mind.

For, lo, the winter is past, the rain is over and gone; The flowers appear on the earth; the time of the singing of birds is come, and the voice of the turtle is heard in our land;
(Song 2:11,12 KJV)

WHAT GOOD IS FAME

What good is fame when life is o'er,
Short lived in all its glory,
When death has spoken, we're soon forgotten,
No more the hero of the story;
It's all so fleeting and yet we strive
To inflate self egos before one dies.

What good is it to be a "star",
To be worshiped and adored by all,
Death knows not one from another,
Patiently sitting, awaiting his call,
Considering not whether rich or poor,
For he takes us all on his V-I-P tour.

God sits above the circle of the earth,
He dooms great men and brings them all to naught,
They barely take root when He blows on them,
Withering their work, wind carrying off what they sought;
The grass withers and flowers fade beneath His breath,
Like fragile man when speaks the silent death.

Death, where is thy sting; grave, where is thy victory;
It's only a change of place for our being;
Absent from the body, we're present with the Lord,
To gaze upon His glory, eyes all-seeing;
And yet, while here below, the banner must be waved,
The harvest is passed, summer has ended, and we are not saved.

While we look not at the things which are seen, but at the things which are not seen: for the things which are seen are temporal; but the things which are not seen are eternal. (II Cor. 4:18 KJV)

THE FALLEN LEAVES

The trees are mostly barren now,
A few little leaves still hang on the bough,
They've tightly clung through rain and dearth,
To the mother tree who's given them birth,
She designed and nourished, a pattern to weave,
But once they've fallen, she cannot retrieve.
Past is the summer, autumn is here,
It's time for a change, another new year.

We can't hang on forever, they cry,
The weather has changed, we too must die,
Our foliage green has now turned brown,
Surely one day we'll fall to the ground,
Just lying around awaiting our turn,
For someone to rake in the fire to burn,
Once so happy, our branches spread wide,
To form a shade from the sun to hide.

Once fallen, if just left alone,
We'd make a brown carpet to tread upon,
To accommodate all, both common and royal,
Then return to the earth, replenish the soil,
When springtime returns and new life begins,
Mother tree will bear new leaves where old ones have been,
And the cycle will start all over again,
The seasons go on, all in God's plan.

"Now learn a lesson from the fig tree. When its buds become tender and its leaves begin to sprout, you know without being told that summer is near. Just so, when you see the events I've described beginning to happen, you can know his return is very near, right at the doors. (Matt 24:32,33 NLT)

GOD'S TOUCH

Just the cool of an early morning breeze,
Dear Lord, to smooth a troubled brow,
Can sweep across and leave its breath,
To sooth my being, I know not how;
The gentle whisper of the wind,
Knowing not from whence it came,
Caresses my cheek with a gentle kiss,
Goes on its way, to come again.

O magnify the Lord with me, and let us exalt his name together. (Ps. 34:3 KJV)

THE ANSWER

Now, my child, I hear your prayer,
Thy voice with questions asking,
Why am I sick, why do I weep,
Why do my pains keep lasting?
What are you trying to tell me Lord,
In answer, please I pray thee,
That I might understand and know,
Thy will sometimes alludes me.

Be patient child, I know it's hard
To walk in faith believing,
When every part of your body aches
With pain you are receiving;
I'm still in charge, I know what's best.
Your character I am building,
Remolding and reshaping you,
Preparing you for yielding.

I want you to be prepared
For life here and hereafter,
I must complete my work in you,
All in my time, slow or faster;
Be not disheartened but trust in me,
With doubts and fears discarded,
You are my child, I'll see you through,
In Heaven, you'll be rewarded.

Hear me, O Lord, hear me, that this people may know that thou art the Lord God, and that thou hast turned their heart back again. (1 Kings 18:37 KJV)

PSALM 114

Long ago the Jews escaped from Egypt
From the land of foreign tongue,
And the lands of Judah and Israel
Became God's new home and kingdom;
The Red Sea saw them coming
And parted with ne'er a loss,
The Jordan river opened up,
A path for them to cross.

What's wrong Red Sea
Why cut yourself in two?
What happened to you Jordan river,
Who held the waters back for you?
Why great mountains, did you skip like little rams,
And you little hills, why did you skip like lambs?

Tremble O Earth at the Lord God's Almighty hand,
Bringing streams of water from the flinty rock
On the way to the promised land.

Reflections

THY

FAITHFUL

SERVANTS

MOSES

A basket sealed with slime and pitch
Was laid on the water bed;
"'Twas time to hide the child inside,
From Herod's wrath," his mother said.

One day when Pharoah's daughter came,
Herself to bathe and sit;
She heard the sound of a baby's cry,
And bade her maids to fetch it.

When she looked inside, her heart aglow,
She claimed him for her own;
His mother in disguise was called
To nurse the baby unknown.

In Egyptian ways this Hebrew child,
Was reared in wealth and fame,
To manhood he would soon become,
To return from which he came.

One day, his Egyptian brother, Moses slew,
And hid him in the sand;
From Pharoah's wrath, he had to flee,
And found a home in Midian.

On the backside of the desert wide,
While tending his flock of sheep,
An angel appeared in a flame of fire
Amidst a bush, he heard him speak.

He heard God's voice call out to him,
He answered, "Lord, here am I,"
"Then take your shoes from off your feet,
'Tis Holy ground you're nigh."

Afraid to look upon Holy God,
His face he hid in fear;
He heard God's voice explain to him,
"My people's cry I hear."

"To Egypt I will send thee,
To set my people free,
To serve me on this mountain top,
To worship me," said He.

But Moses said, "God, who am I?
Your name, what will it be?"
And God replied, "Just tell them,
I Am that I Am has sent thee."

"But God, I am so slow of speech,
My eloquence I deny,"
"Your brother shall your spokesman be,"
He heard God's voice reply.

"Now take your rod and cast it down,
A serpent shall it be,
Pick up the tail within your hand,
The rod again you'll see."

"Into your bosom, now thrust your hand,
A leprous skin emerging,
Now take this, a sign from me,
And be thou not discouraging."

With Aaron by his side he went,
His rod beside him so,
The message loud and clear to speak,
"Let my people go."

He found the task before him grave,
Enslaved the people perished,
From burdens great upon their backs,
No future hope, they cherished.

With bricks to make from dawn to dusk,
He found the people broken,
God heard their cry and sent these words,
To Pharoah they were spoken.

"God said to let my people go,
And harden not your heart,
Or plagues to you I will bestow,
My judgement to impart."

But Pharoah would not let them go,
And God rained from on high,
Bloody water, darkness, locusts, boils, and frogs,
And hail and lice and flies.

And then God sent his greatest plague,
The death of all firstborn,
And Pharoah's house did not escape,
At midnight, he did mourn.

God told them all to take a lamb,
Unblemished it shall be,
And wipe the door posts of each house,
This blood, a sign for me.

When I shall see the blood displayed,
I will then pass over you,
Pharoah's mind I then will change,
My will for him to do.

Now roast the lamb, let none remain,
With haste, as thou art able,
Unleavened bread and bitter herbs
Shall be upon your table.

This memorial feast forever keep
Throughout your generations,
Unleavened bread for seven days,
And the passover celebration.

So carry your clothes upon your back,
With borrowed silver and gold;
Six hundred thousand men in all,
Shall march your army bold.

When thou has reached the promised land,
Feet planted firmly on the sod,
When thou hast eaten, are fat and full,
Do not forsake your God.

No house escaped so great a cry,
All Egypt was a mourning;
But for the ones who had the blood
On the lintel posts adorning.

So Moses began his wilderness march,
God's protection his desire,
By day He gave a pillar of cloud,
By night, a pillar of fire.

They reached the sea, the great Red Sea,
He knew not what to do,
"Lift up your rod," God said, "your hand stretched high,
And I will fight for you."

A strong east wind blew all night long
Across the great Red Sea,
The waters divided and formed a wall;
The Israelites marched free.

The Egyptians came, the waters returned,
Dead bodies ashore to remain;
Then sang the children of Israel,
The Lord God is his name.

Now God, I've marched the wilderness route,
With Moses as my guide,
I've suffered with him and felt his pain,
And tasted sweet victories inside.

The miracles with which you blessed them
Are too many to recall,
The waters made sweet from a branch of a limb,
Their clothes not tattered at all.

How they fussed and grumbled and murmured so,
For melons, garlic, and leeks, they said,
How you provided their every need,
With manna and quail you fed.

And when Moses ascended to Mt. Sinai,
At your command to stay
With you for 40 days and nights,
Your words he did obey.

With Thy finger, you wrote the laws,
On tablets of stone engraved;
The mountains did quake with billows of smoke,
The thunderings and lightnings raved.

When Moses desired to see his God,
Yet no man could live and be,
How with your hand, you hid his face,
Only your back to see.

When Moses descended the mountain top,
They were worshiping the golden calf,
How 3,000 men were slain that day,
And the tablets were broken in wrath.

How you gave the instructions for making,
Enveloping every minute detail,
Tabernacle, ark, mercy seat, curtains, and courts,
Altar, breastplates, garments, and veil.

I cried dear God when Moses prayed,
To ask you for a favor,
To let him lead across the Jordan,
The promised land to savor.

You answered him, "Speak no more to me,
For Canaan thou shalt not enter,
But get yourself up on the Pisgah Peak,
One last look I'll render.

"You sanctified me not before the people,
To speak to the rock, without doubt,
But with your rod, you smote it twice,
And the waters came gushing out.

"So here on Mt. Nebo thou shalt die,
In the land of Moab rest,
Thy servant Joshua shall take your place,
To Canaan land be blessed."

There Moses found death, was buried by God,
His sepulchre hidden from view,
But in the deepest recess of God's heart,
He holds the secret anew.

And there arose not a prophet since in Israel like unto Moses, whom the Lord knew face to face, (Deut. 34:10 KJV)

SAMSON

God let Israel be ruled by Judges,
Because of their turning from Him,
Many were chosen from the different tribes,
For years, Judges ruled over them.

Once again Israel sinned against God,
Turned to the gods of the heathen, and
God sent an angel to announce a birth
To a woman from the tribe of Dan.

"Even though you've been barren for years," he said,
"You shall conceive and bring forth a son,
Drink no wine, eat no food that's not kosher,
Until this promise from God is come."

"Your son's hair must never be cut,
He will be a Nazarite from the womb,
God has chosen him a special servant to be,
To save His people from doom."

The woman ran and told her husband,
"An angel of the Lord has been here,
I don't know his name or where he's from,
But he said not to drink wine or beer."

Then her husband prayed unto the Lord,
"Let the man of God come again here,
Give us instructions about the child you give,"
God heard, the angel once more did appear.

Then the husband said to the angel,
"Tell us how to raise the baby when born,"
The angel replied, "Follow all my instructions,
And his hair is not to be shorn."

Then he asked, "But what is your name,
We'll want to tell others of your task,"
The angel replied, "Bring an offering unto the Lord,
My name is a secret, don't ask."

They offered a burnt sacrifice unto the Lord,
To thank the Lord was their desire,
But as they watched the flame go up,
The angel ascended up in the fire.

So Samson was born, grew into a man,
Fell in love with a heathen girl,
His parents objected to his choice,
Not knowing God's hand would unfurl.

One day as Samson was on the road,
He was attacked by a young lion,
With only the spirit of God as his weapon,
He ripped the jaws apart in no time.

A few days later, he returned to the carcass,
Found bees inside making honey,
So he reached inside and drew out some,
Walked down the road filling his tummy.

At the wedding feast, he told his friends,
"I have a riddle for you," said he,
"If you can solve it in seven days,
Sixty robes I'll give you, if not, you give me."

"Food came out of the eater, sweetness from the strong,"
The young men strove hard to achieve their desire,
But on the fourth day, they threatened his wife,
If the answer, she did not acquire.

On the seventh day, she coaxed the answer
From Samson, and gave to the young men,
Samson angrily went out and slew thirty,
Gave their robes to those who did win.

So Samson got angry, left his new wife,
Returned to mom and dad again,
When he later returned to reclaim his wife,
He found her married to his best man.

So Samson went out, caught 300 foxes,
Tied their tails together in pairs all around,
Lit a torch between each pair of them,
Burned their fields of grain to the ground.

Now the Philistines were angry, their crops were gone,
Samson ran to a cave to hide,
When the men of Judah came to turn him in,
They brought new ropes for him to be tied.

When they arrived with Samson all tied up,
The Philistines shouted with glee,
But the strength of the Lord came upon him,
The ropes snapped like thread, Samson went free.

He picked up a jawbone of an ass lying near,
Slew thousands of Philistines by his hand,
Samson judged Israel the next twenty years,
But the Philistines controlled all the land.

One day Samson fell in love with Delilah,
They bribed her to find his strength to contain,
So she begged him to tell her his secret,
So the Philistines could bind him in chains.

"If I were tied with seven leather bow strings,"
He said, "All my strength would cease,"
So when asleep, she tied him up,
He awoke, broke the strings with ease.

Again, he said, “If you tie me with ropes,
I’ll be as weak as others in the land,"
And as he slept, she tied him again,
The ropes broke like spider webs in his hand.

The third time she asked, "What is your strength?"
He said, "Weave my hair into your loom,”
She did just that, called out his name,
He yanked out his hair and fled from the room.

She nagged and nagged at him for days,
‘Til at last she weakened his will,
He confessed to her, "I'm a Nazarite from birth,
If you cut my hair, my strength will be nil.”

So she lulled him to sleep one more time,
Brought in a barber to cut off his hair,
And when he awoke, he had no strength,
The power of the Lord no longer to share.

The Philistines grabbed him, gauged out his eyes,
Took him off and bound him with chains,
They took him to prison to grind out the grain,
But soon his hair started to grow out again.

The Philistines decided to give a big party
To praise god Dagon for what he had done,
Half drunk, they shouted, "Bring Samson out,
With him, we’ll have lots of fun."

Samson was brought forth from the prison,
Stood between two pillars supporting the roof,
"Place my hands against the two pillars," he said,
"So I can rest, my body to sooth."

Then Samson prayed to his Lord Jehovah,
"Please strengthen just one more time," he sighs,
"So I can pay back the Philistines,
For the less of at least one of my eyes."

He pushed with all of his strength and might,
"Let me die with the Philistines," he cried,
And the temple crashed down upon them all,
So Samson and thousands of Philistines died.

You are my King and my God. You command victories for your people. Only by your power can we push back our enemies; only in your name can we trample our foes.
(Ps. 44:4,5 NLT)

QUEEN ESTHER

A feast was given by the Persian King,
Seven days of celebration to all,
To drink 'til full the royal wine,
Everyone, both great and small.

On the seventh day when the heart of
The king was merry with wine,
He summoned forth Vashti the Queen,
To display her beauty sublime.

But the queen refused the king's command,
His lust to satisfy;
His princes then trying to sooth,
Said, "What can be done to Queen Vashti?

"Let there be a decree from the king,
A published law, unchangeable to say,
That Queen Vashti can no longer appear,
Her estate be another's joy," said they.

Later, the king's wrath appeased,
The servants to please him replied,
"Let young virgins be sought throughout the land,
To take the queen's place," they cried.

There was a certain Jew, Mordecai by name,
From Jerusalem, a captive been taken,
Who had brought along Esther, an orphan girl,
A kinsman, he had not forsaken.

This maiden girl, so beautiful and fair,
Was summoned for the king to eye;
He set the royal crown upon her head,
Made her queen instead of Vashti.

The king promoted his servant Haman,
For all to reverence and bow,
But Mordecai, the Jew, refused to obey,
And in wrath, Haman did vow.

With his plan to slay all the Jews,
Haman hurriedly went to the king;
The king responded to his demands,
Sealed the agreement with his ring.

Every Jew, both young and old alike,
Must be destroyed, the law be kept;
But when Mordecai heard the news,
In sackcloth and ashes, he wept.

This law was told to Queen Esther,
Of the Jews' fasting, weeping and wailing;
Mordecai demanded she go to the king,
To beg mercy for the Jews' travailing.

"I can't," she said, "Go before my king,
Without being summoned about,
There is a law to put one to death,
Unless the golden scepter he holds out."

"If I've not been called in thirty days
To appear before the king," she cried;
"Perhaps you're here for such a time as this,
Do you think you alone will survive?" he replied.

"Neither eat nor drink for three days," said she,
"We'll fast for my people I cherish,
Against the law, I'll go to the king,
And if I perish, I perish."

The king was sitting on his royal throne,
When Esther the queen appeared;
The king held out the golden scepter,
She touched the tip and neared.

"What wilt thou, Esther my queen,"
He asked, "What is thy request,
Whatever your wish shall be yours," he said,
"The half of my kingdom, your behest."

"I have prepared a banquet," she said,
"For you and Haman to come,
I will at that time reveal unto you,
My request I pray will be done."

That very night, the king could not sleep,
"Bring forth the historical records," he saith,
And as they read the book, they found
That Mordecai had saved the king from death.

The king then asked, "What has been done
To honor this man for this deed?"
"Nothing at all, sir," they replied,
"But there should be such a decree."

"Adorn him in my royal apparel," he said,
"Let him ride on my royal horse,
Place the royal crown upon his head."
Haman thought he was the one, of course.

When Haman found out that Mordecai
Was the honored one to be,
He quickly plotted all the Jews' death,
But for Mordecai, a gallows made he.

Then the king and Haman went in to the feast,
Which Esther the Queen had prepared,
With trembling voice, she made her request,
That the life of the Jews be spared.

"Why, who could ever do such a thing?"
The king asked, "Who could be so callous?"
"It is that wicked Haman," Esther replied,
So Haman was hung on his gallows.

Queen Esther revealed for the very first time
That she and Mordecai were both Jews,
The king made Mordecai Prime Minister,
Reversed the law that was issued.

A new law was written, the Jews united,
All those who hated were slain,
Thousands of enemies were destroyed that day,
Peace and harmony again did reign.

The Jews declared a two-day feast,
For praise and gifts of giving,
Remembering how their sorrows
Had turned into joyous living.

For on the day that Haman cast lot,
To see what day he'd slay them;
"We'll celebrate through years to come,"
They said, "This annual festival of Purim."

Therefore the Jews of the villages, that dwelt in the unwalled towns, made the fourteenth day of the month Adar a day of gladness and feasting, and a good day, and of sending portions one to another. (Esther 9:19 KJV)

ZACCHEUS

Now Zaccheus resided in Jericho,
Was short of stature, you know;
Collecting taxes, his days were spent
In serving the Roman Government.

Zaccheus heard the news one day,
Jesus was passing that way;
The crowd was pushing and shoving so,
How could he see, where could he go?

A thought occurred inside his head,
"I know what I shall do," he said,
"I'll climb right up that sycamore tree,
Then I shall clearly see."

So he perched himself a way up high
On a limb, he found nearby,
He heard the shouts; he heard the noise,
Undisturbed, he was safely poised.

When Jesus passed beneath the tree,
He paused, and looking up to see,
Called, "Zaccheus, I'm going to your house today,
So hasten on down," he heard Him say.

Now Zaccheus had become a very rich man,
Collecting more taxes than was the plan;
Murmuring, the people asked, "How can this be,
That Jesus would dine with a sinner as he."

So touched by Jesus' loving concern,
His guilt within his soul did burn,
And with these words, he did assure,
"Half of my goods Lord, I'll give to the poor."

"And whatever deceitful gains this day,
I now restore fourfold to pay."
"Zaccheus," replied Jesus, without delay,
"Salvation has come to your house today."

The wicked borroweth, and payeth not again: but the righteous sheweth mercy, and giveth. (Ps. 37:21 KJV)

LAZARUS

Lazarus, in the little town of Bethany lived
With two sisters, Martha and Mary,
When Lazarus came down very sick one day,
In another town, Jesus did tarry.

So they sent Him an urgent message,
Your friend, Lazarus, is very ill;
But Jesus lingered two days more,
Before His miracle He'd fulfill.

Then He said to His disciples,
"To Judea we must now go,"
"But the Jews are out to kill you there,"
They replied, "You know that this is so."

"Our friend Lazarus has gone to sleep,
And I must go to awaken him,
We have twelve hours to safely walk,
Before our steps at night grow dim."

"If Lazarus is having a good night's sleep,
That means he is well," they said,
"For your sake, I'm glad I was not there,
For you see, Lazarus is dead."

When they arrived near Bethany,
Jesus was told Lazarus had been buried four days;
When Martha heard Jesus was coming nigh,
She ran to meet Him, as always.

"Sir," she said, "If you had been here,
My brother would not have died,
And even now, it's not too late,"
"Your brother will live again," He replied.

"I know that he will rise again
On that great resurrection day,"
"Martha, I am the one who raises the dead
And gives them life," she heard Him say.

Then Martha returned and told Mary,
"Jesus is here, He wants to see you,"
So Mary and some of the Jews with her,
Hurried out to see Jesus too.

Mary fell down at Jesus' feet,
"Had you been here, he would still be alive,"
When Jesus saw them weeping and wailing so,
Compassionate tears filled His eyes.

They came to the tomb where Lazarus laid,
A heavy stone across the door;
"Roll the stone aside," He told them,
"Only believe, I've said it before."

"Lazarus, come out," He shouted,
He came forth, hands and feet bound,
"Unwrap him, let him go," He cried,
And immediately, he was unwound.

Many of the Jewish leaders there that day,
Who saw the miracles Jesus had done,
Believed on Him as their Messiah,
But doubt still filled the hearts of some.

Now according to old tradition,
But the Bible does not so claim,
Lazarus was thirty years old when restored to life,
And lived thirty years after again.

Jesus said unto her, I am the resurrection, and the life; he that believeth in me, though he were dead, yet shall he live:
(John 11:25 KJV)

JONAH

Now the word of the Lord came to Jonah,
"I need a man to go to Nineveh," He said,
"For their wickedness has come up before me,"
From the presence of God, Jonah fled.

So he found a ship down in Jeppa,
And Jonah paid his fare;
But God sent a great wind into the sea,
With the waves tossing here and there.

They were afraid and to lighten the load,
They cast their wares into the deep;
Then each prayed to his God for help,
But Jonah lay fast asleep.

They said, "Arise, call on your God,
Perhaps he will hear and make well,"
They then cast lots for the cause of their fate,
And on Jonah, the lot fell.

"Tell us," they said, "Who are you?
What evil have you done?
Why have you caused this upon us?
What is your job, from where do you come?"

"I am a Hebrew, and I fear the Lord,
Who made the sea and the land," said he.
"What shall we do with you?" they asked,
"Take me and cast into the sea."

Nevertheless, the men rowed hard;
They could not bring the ship to land;
They cried, "Lord, we beseech thee,
Don't let us perish because of this man."

They took up Jonah and cast him forth
Into the raging sea,
Into the belly of a great big fish,
For three days and nights to be.

Then Jonah prayed unto the Lord,
Out of the belly of the fish, he said,
"The depth closed round about me,
And the weeds wrapped around my head."

"Thou hast cast me down into the deep,
Into the midst of the sea;
I went down to the bottom of the mountains,
The billows and waves passed over me."

Then Jonah's heart fainted within him,
And the Lord gave the command;
Unto the fish, he told him,
"Vomit out Jonah on dry land."

Now God spoke to Jonah the second time,
"To Nineveh I bid thee gone,
And warn the people that in forty days,
To repent or be overthrown."

The King of Nineveh decreed a fast,
In sackcloth and ashes repent;
The people turned from their evil ways,
God's forgiveness to them was sent.

But Jonah was angry and said to God,
"Thou has kindness and mercy to give,
I beseech thee to take my life from me,
It is better to die than to live."

Jonah went outside the city,
And made himself a booth,
To sleep beneath the shadow thereof;
His grief he tried to sooth.

While waiting to see the city's fate,
The Lord God prepared a gourd
To grow up over Jonah's head,
And his gladness within him soared.

The next morning though, God prepared a worm
To eat the gourd nearby,
When the hot sun beat upon Jonah's head,
He fainted and wished to die.

God said, "You do well to be angry and pity the gourd,
You did no labor, nor made it grow there,
It grew in a night and perished in a night;
Jonah, should I not Nineveh spare?"

When my soul fainted within me I remembered the Lord: and my prayer came in unto thee, into thine holy temple.
(Jonah 2:7 KJV)

JOSEPH

I cried, dear Lord, at Joseph's fate,
The favorite of his father,
Who, into the pit his brothers threw,
It seemed with ne'er a bother.

Sold for a slave when strangers neared,
To Egypt they did take him;
In Pharoah's court, he found himself,
With decisions wise, he pleased them.

In later years, his brothers came,
In famine they did hunger,
And in disguise, he sold them grain,
Inquiring as to their number.

Your father, is he still alive?
Do you have yet a brother?
And then made known himself to them,
And wept with one another.

Be not thou grieved nor anger more,
For the deed that thou has done;
For God does rule this heart of mine,
A ruler I've become.

With haste, go fetch your father here,
In Goshen shalt he dwell,
This evil deed that thou has done,
To me, God meant it well.

At age one hundred ten he died,
With only one request,
When God shall bring you out of this land,
There carry my bones to rest.

Now Israel loved Joseph more than all his children, because he was the son of his old age: and he made him a coat of many colours. (Gen. 37:3 KJV)

JOHN THE BAPTIST

There was in the days of Herod the king,
A couple well stricken in years;
Zaccharias and Elizabeth by name
Prayed daily for a child, it appears.

Now righteous before the Lord were they,
Blameless before Him unswerved;
Faithful in duty his office as priest,
Zaccharias in the temple served.

While praying one day at the altar,
An angel appeared at his side;
His spirit was fearful and troubled,
And wondered what his presence implied.

The angel then said unto him,
"Fear not, your prayer has been heard anon,
Elizabeth shall surely bear thee a son,
And thou shalt call his name "John".

"He shall be great in the sight of the Lord,
Neither wine nor strong drink imbibe,
He shall be filled with the Holy Ghost
From the womb," the angel replied.

Zaccharias then said to the angel,
"How can this be, how shall I know
That God has chosen to bless us,
For I am too old and my wife also?"

"I am the angel Gabriel," he said,
"In the presence of God I stand,
This message from Him I bring you,
Glad tidings throughout the land.

"Thou shalt be dumb, unable to speak,
Because you believe not my word;
Until these things have come to pass,
No sound from your lips shall be heard."

The people outside became troubled,
He tarried too long, they believed;
And when he appeared and could not speak,
A vision from God, they perceived.

It came to pass, a child was born,
Family and friends rejoicing were led;
"Zaccharias," they shouted, "His name shall be,"
"Not so, 'Tis John," his mother said.

"But why," they cried, all in one accord,
"You have no kin by that name," they respond;
Asking the father what he would be called,
On a tablet, he wrote the word "John".

Then at that moment, his tongue was loosed,
The word spread across the country;
Those who heard it wondered aloud,
What manner of child shall this be?

Then Zaccharias began to prophesy,
Filled with the Holy Ghost, power and vim;
"This child shall go before the face of the Lord,
To prepare the way before Him."

The child grew and waxed strong in spirit,
In the desert, he made his retreat;
He wore camel's hair and a leathern girdle,
With locusts and wild honey his meat.

John preached in the wilderness around Jordan,
Be baptized, of your sins repent,
As foretold by Isaiah the prophet,
A forerunner for Christ, John was sent.

The Jews hearing of John's preaching,
And jealous of all his fame,
Resentful of all his following,
Sent priests to inquire his name.

"Tell us," they asked, "Who art thou?"
"I am not the Christ," he confessed;
"I am the forerunner of the one to follow,
A voice crying in the wilderness."

When John baptized Jesus in the river Jordan,
The spirit descended in the shape of a dove,
And a voice was heard from Heaven,
"In thee I am well pleased, my Son beloved."

Now John had warned King Herod
That he had done wrong, he saith,
In marrying his brother's wife, Herodias,
So the king longed to put John to death.

On Herod's birthday, a party was held,
He beckoned Salome to dance;
She pleased him so, her desire he swore,
To the half of his kingdom per chance.

Being instructed afore by her mother,
John's head in a charger, she demanded,
He saddened, but an oath he had given,
Only one thing to do, he commanded.

He sent and beheaded John in the prison,
To the damsel, his head was brought;
She presented the gift to her mother,
Who received the desire she had sought.

John's voice is still heard in the wilderness,
His message not stilled with his breath;
A life marked by humility, denial, and courage,
A willing victim to prison and death.

His message still loudly ringing,
Proclaimed throughout the years,
Repent, believe in Jesus,
The One to come is here.

But when Herod heard thereof, he said, It is John, whom I beheaded: he is risen from the dead. (Mark 6:16 KJV)

DAVID ANOINTED AS KING

Saul, Israel's first anointed king,
Disobeyed God, more sorrows to bring;
God sent Samuel, the prophet, to notify Saul
That the kingdom under him would ultimately fall.

Samuel mourned for the downfall of Saul the king,
But God said, "Take a vial of olive oil and bring
To Bethlehem, anoint a future king for me,
Out of the family of Jesse, I want him to be."

Samuel replied, "Lord, King Saul will be angry with me,
He will have me killed, my life to be,"
But God answered, "A sacrifice you must make,
Ask Jesse and his family to come and partake."

When the purification rites had all been done,
And Jesse had attended with his seven sons,
Each son was presented to Saul, so dear,
But still the right one did not appear.

Samuel said, "Lord, this must surely be the one,"
As each presentation before him was done;
God said, "I don't look on the outward appearance part,
Samuel, I look only into man's heart."

Then Samuel said to Jesse, "God has chosen none,
Tell me, are these all, is there not another son?"
Jesse replied, "There is one yet, the youngest I keep
Out in the field tending the sheep."

Samuel said, "Send at once for him to come in,
Until he arrives, our meal will not begin."
When the fine looking, ruddy-faced boy appeared before them,
The Lord said, "Samuel, this is the one, anoint him."

Upon young David's head, Samuel did pour
The anointed oil he had in store,
But the Spirit of God then left King Saul,
And a tormenting spirit of fear did fall.

They cried, "We need a harpist who comes and serves,
Who calms and soothes his troubled nerves."
They asked around and found the one to bring,
Was Jesse's son, David, to serve the King?

Now the Philistines had mustered an army for war,
They had Goliath, a giant from Gath, their star;
He was powerful, measuring over nine feet tall,
And King Saul's army was afraid of them all.

Young David said, "Don't worry about Goliath more,
For I've killed lions and bears before,
Don't fear Goliath, though he a giant be,
For the Lord my God will be with me."

Now King Saul offered David his armor to wear,
But David refused the offer so rare,
He picked up five smooth stones in his bag to bring,
Started off with his shepherd's staff and sling.

He met Goliath, who wanted to know,
"You mean they've sent a young boy with no bow."
David cried, "I've come in the name of the Lord," so
He reached for one stone from his bag and let go.

The stone hit the forehead of the giant,
He fell on his face, so self reliant.
So David killed with a sling and a stone,
The army was beaten, their confidence gone.

Though David would wait years to become king,
To replace Saul, great leadership to bring,
He served King Saul so loyal and true,
As commander in chief, his popularity grew.

But King Saul became jealous of David, his foe,
For all Israel and Judah loved him so,
And when the evil spirits tormented King Saul,
He ranted and raved like a madman to all.

One day while David was playing his harp,
To calm the tormenting spirit of Saul's heart,
A spear was hurled from the hand of King Saul,
David stepped aside, the spear hit the wall.

Saul's young son Jonathan and David lovingly
Swore to each other, a blood brother to be,
They made a pact of the love they felt,
Jonathan gave him his sword, bow, and belt.

King Saul tried to kill David, and then
Forcing him to flee, ere his life to end,
David lived in a cave where he did hide,
But the Lord his God was on his side.

Soon David had a band of followers grand,
God delivered Saul many times to his hand,
But David bowed low before his command,
Saying "I cannot slay God's chosen man."

On the day of battle when the Philistines came,
King Saul and Jonathan both were slain,
So David was crowned King, all Israel proclaimed,
And for forty years altogether he reigned.

And may your name be established and honored forever so that all the world will say, 'The Lord Almighty is God over Israel!' And may the dynasty of your servant David be established in your presence. (1Chron. 17:24 NLT)

SAUL'S (PAUL'S) CONVERSION

One day, Saul, a Jew from Tarsus,
A strict Pharisee of the law,
Was granted the permission to bring in
All the disciples of the Lord he saw.

Now Saul was a very zealous Jew,
A Hebrew of the Hebrews;
He continued to search and oppress the saints,
With threatenings and slaughters to pursue.

At noon one day while on his journey,
To Damascus he was to go,
A light from Heaven surrounded him,
And a voice he did not know.

He fell to the ground and heard a voice,
"Saul, Saul, why do you persecute me?"
And Saul replied, "Who art thou Lord,
That I might know thee?"

"I am Jesus, whom you persecute,
Arise, into the city go;"
When Saul arose, he could not see,
Blindness he was to know.

The men with Saul were speechless,
Hearing a voice but seeing no man;
Trembling with astonishment,
They led Saul by the hand.

For three days without his sight,
Saul did neither eat nor drink;
His zeal was fast diminishing,
Sorrow and remorse piercing deep.

God spoke in a vision to Ananias,
"Arise, go to the street called Straight,
Call for a man of Taurus,
For I have told him to wait."

Ananias replied, "I've heard of him, Lord,
He's persecuted all the while,"
"He is a chosen vessel to me," said God,
"To bear my name to the Gentiles."

So Ananias, a devout man, found Saul,
Laying hands on him did tell,
"Brother Saul, now receive your sight,"
Something fell from his eyes as scales.

He immediately arose, was strengthened,
Baptized and filled with the Holy Ghost,
Preaching in all the synagogues,
Christ the Son of God to boast.

Though persecuted, imprisoned, stoned for dead,
His love for God to share;
With burning zeal, he served Him well,
Tribulations and trials to bear.

"I've fought a good fight, I've finished the course,"
Paul, at his death could say,
"And a crown of righteousness awaits me,
Which the Lord will give the last day."

For I will shew him how great things he must suffer for my name's sake. (Acts 9:16 KJV)

PAUL'S LETTER TO PHILEMON

Dear Philemon –

I greet you my fellow worker
And the church that meets in your home,
To those, like myself, soldiers of the cross,
I send you my greetings from Rome.

May God our Father and the Lord Jesus Christ
Give you his blessings and peace;
I keep hearing of how you are sharing your faith,
And I pray that your trust will increase.

I've gained joy and comfort from your love,
And know of your kindness to others,
But I have a favor to ask of you
For the sake of my friend and brother.

I beg you to show kindness to my child
Onesimus, whom I've won to the Lord;
I'm an old man now here in jail,
I'm bound with chains and with cord.

I know he's not been much use to you lately,
And I hate to see him depart,
But I'm sending him on back to you now,
And with him comes my own heart.

I really wanted to keep him with me,
But not without your consent,
I didn't want you to be kind because you had to,
But because you willingly gave your assent.

I know he ran away as a slave from you
Without your approval or desire,
But now he is a brother in Christ,
And I'm asking you please to rehire.

If I am your friend, please welcome him,
The same welcome you would give me,
If he has harmed or stolen from you,
Charge to my account, I'll pay the fee.

But remember, you owe me your very soul,
So give me joy with this loving deed,
And my weary heart will praise the Lord,
For your forgiving spirit we need.

Please keep a guest room ready for me,
For I hope God will answer your prayer,
To let me soon come to visit you,
My love for Christ to share.

My fellow prisoner here with me
Is in jail for preaching Christ too,
My fellow workers send you their love,
And blessings of our Lord be upon you.

From Paul, in jail for preaching Good News,
And Brother Timothy send greetings to you.

Your own soul is nourished when you are kind, but you destroy yourself when you are cruel. (Prov. 11:17 NLT)

CONVERSION OF THE GENTILES

There was a man from Caesarea,
Cornelius was his name,
An officer in the Roman guard,
A generous and prayerful man he became.

One afternoon around three o'clock.
While awake, he had a vision,
An angel of the Lord appeared unto him,
Sent by God to him with a mission.

"Cornelius," the angel said unto him,
He answered, "What do you want, Sir?"
"Send men to Joppa for a man named Peter,
He is staying with Simon, the tanner."

The next day as they were nearing the city,
Peter went up on the house top to pray,
It was noon and he was hungry,
While waiting for lunch, a trance came his way.

He saw the sky open and a great canvas sheet
Was suspended by all four corners so neat,
It settled to the ground with all sorts of animals,
Foods forbidden by the Jews to eat.

He heard a voice, "Rise, Peter, kill and eat,"
Peter said, "Never, Lord, I've never eaten such things,
These are all forbidden by the Jewish law,"
The voice said, "Don't contradict God, eat what God brings."

This vision he saw was repeated three times,
Then the sheet was pulled up to heaven again,
Peter was baffled, what does this mean,
For to him, all those things were unclean.

Just then, the men from Caesarea arrived,
The Holy Spirit said to Peter, “Go down,
Three men are at the gate to see you,
Go with them, I’ve sent them to your town.”

Peter went down, “I’m the one you’re looking for,”
He said, “Tell me, what do you want of me?”
They explained to him how Cornelius had seen
In a vision these things to be.

The next morning Peter accompanied the men
To the house where Cornelius did wait,
Together with relatives and many close friends,
This vision from God to relate.

When Peter arrived, Cornelius fell to the floor
To worship Peter whom God had sent,
Peter said, “Stand up Cornelius, I’m not a God,”
Cornelius arose, into the room they went.

Peter began, “It’s against the law for me to come
Into the house of a Gentile man,
But God has shown to me in a vision,
That all men are equal under His hand.”

Cornelius told Peter of his vision and said,
“We are waiting for what you have to say,
We know that God has brought you here,
We’re so glad that you came today.”

Then Peter opened his mouth and said,
“Of a truth, Jesus is Lord of all,
For God is no respecter of persons,
He’s available to all who call.

"You've heard how Jesus was anointed with power,
Who went about healing and doing good,
We are witnesses to all the things He did
In Jerusalem, and the things which He withstood.

"How they slew Him and hanged Him on a tree,
How God raised Him on the third day," he said,
"We witnessed all these things about Him,
We ate and drank with Him after He arose from the dead.

"He told us to preach to all people,
That He's the Judge of the quick and the dead,
And that whosoever believeth in Him,
Shall receive remission of sins," he said.

While Peter was speaking all of these words,
The Holy Spirit fell upon them all,
The Jews who came with Peter were astonished
That on the Gentiles too, the Spirit did fall.

They spoke with tongues and magnified God,
"They've received the Spirit as well as we,
Can anyone deny baptism to them," Peter asked,
"Be baptized in the name of the Lord," said he.

Now tradition tells us that when Peter died,
He said with a voice strong and lucid,
"Please hang me upside down on the cross,
I'm not worthy to hang as my Lord did."

Even the righteousness of God which is by faith of Jesus Christ unto all and upon all them that believe: for there is no difference: For all have sinned, and come short of the glory of God; (Rom. 3:22,23 KJV)

Reflections

PAST

KEEPSAKES

A TRIBUTE TO FIVE

So long ago, it seems so now,
When I was but a wee one,
The memories faded dim somehow
Of sorrow, where there is none.

Shortly after I was born,
I was the fifth, you see, in line,
My sister small with hair so red,
Died, a lovely child of five, they said.

Then God took papa home from us,
Almost too young to remember,
But coming down that dusty road,
A big black hearse so long and slender.

So mama, left with six less one,
With only a team of mules and wagon,
And a little farming land to rent,
We had no room for braggin'.

Hard times upon us, we endured,
The scrubbing, ironing, and all the fuss,
I'm sure at times though my mama worried,
That maybe God had forsaken us.

To share our home and all our woes,
Mama's life, she was to fix,
She found a husband with an only daughter,
So now the five of us again were six.

Six girls in all, can you imagine,
All poured into one mixture,
I'm sure they yearned for daytime spent,
And the quiet of sleep an elixir.

All six of us are still alive,
Senior citizens though we be,
Though mom and dad have long been gone,
We still are one big family.

Now the elder sister in our group,
A longing for knowledge she yearned,
Ambitious and with the witty remark,
With patience and endurance, she learned.

The next to the older down the line,
Hard work, she's not ashamed,
Unselfish and kind her nature is,
To criticize others, she's not blamed.

One of the middle ones so to speak,
Her personality, the friendlier,
Her care for others and helping hands,
Are always there when you need her.

The next middle one, number four in line,
Her raven hair her beauty,
Her openness, humor, mixed with charm,
Have endured her heart to many.

Now in this spot I would appear,
If I so modestly wanted,
But since unfair to rate myself,
My appraisal goes unflaunted.

The last, the younger of the lot,
Eager to help if you call,
Considerate, practical, warm at heart,
Probably the fairest of us all.

God gave me these siblings five,
All sisters and no brothers,
I love them each with a special love,
I'd trade them not for others.

Lo, children are an heritage of the Lord: and the fruit of the womb is his reward. (Ps. 127:3 KJV)

HAVE YOU EVER

Have you ever given your heart
Till death, with one depart,
Well, I have.
Have you ever been disappointed with life,
Amid all the pains and earthly strifes,
Well, I have.

Have you ever struggled with fear and doubt,
Not knowing when things would turn about,
Well, I have.
Have you ever asked God to empathize
With you when you suffer and agonize,
Well, I have.

Have you ever asked God to live within you,
To forgive your sins, His will to do,
Well, I have.
Have you ever received His gift selected,
Of the crucified Christ, buried and resurrected,
Well, I have.

Have you ever blessed His name and praised
In song and prayer with voice upraised,
Well, I have.
Have you ever found peace and contentment within,
Serving your Master, Saviour and Friend,
Well, I have, yes, I have, I have.

And again, Praise the Lord, all ye Gentiles; and laud him, all ye people. (Rom. 15:11 KJV)

THE WONDER OF GOD'S LOVE

As I sit, dear Lord, alone with thee,
In quiet solitude living,
I lift mine eyes and see thy beauty
In nature's mystery giving;
The birds so busily chirping a tune,
In morning songs so fleeting,
The trees that stand so tall and wave,
Nodding their heads in greeting;
The grass beneath my tender feet,
Like cushions of velvet spreading,
So innocently provides for me,
Carpets for my feet in treading.

The little flowers in sweet aroma,
Providing beauty so unassuming,
They are so pure and knowing not,
Of their glory arrayed in blooming;
O, how I'd love to sweep them all
In arms of loving rapture,
But knowing that their life would end,
Much faster if I capture;
So I'll just gaze and marvel yet,
Of thy goodness, my heart to ponder,
I'll feast mine eyes on what you give,
And drink my fill in wonder.

What is man, that thou art mindful of him? and the son of man, that thou visitest him? (Ps. 8:4 KJV)

IN SILENT COMMUNION

When twilight comes in early morn
So innocently arriving,
Before awakening of earthly sounds
And voices all a sighing;
And flittering and fluttering of winged birds
Begin their songs of greeting,
I sit in awe, commune with God,
Entwined our spirits meeting.

No spoken words encase my lips,
Silent thought traverses,
Words without form in secret lie,
My soul with God immerses;
With calming and with soothing tones
Ever so gently drifting,
Like vapors from the misty sky,
His message so uplifting.

And ere the day begins to dawn,
And life begins a stirring,
My worries left from day before
Are slowly, slowly blurring;
The old becomes the new again,
Transposed and intermarried,
My fears and doubts lying deep
In silent repose are buried.

I call to remembrance my song in the night: I commune with mine own heart: and my spirit made diligent search.
(Ps. 77:6 KJV)

THE NEW MAYOR

One morn in church where aft I went,
Sat a lovely woman long side of a gent;
Sitting regally erect, so polished and prim,
I thought it my duty to welcome them.

She, a bright red dress, flowers not a few,
He, properly attired in a suit of blue;
Strangers no doubt, for I knew them all,
For I'd been in office 10 years come next fall.

No need of suspicion with doubts and fears,
Honor and respected by all of my peers,
With excellent service my appointment secure,
A man of experience, no mere amateur.

So with sermon all over and benediction said,
And grandiose words floating round in my head,
I greeted him warmly, extending my hand,
And welcomed them to our town Melody Land.

He arose so politely and with eloquent voice,
Introduced the lady as his dear wife Lois;
"I'm the town mayor," said I, beginning to speak,
"Morning Sir," interrupted he, "I'm the new mayor
beginning next week."

The thing that I dreaded had now come to pass,
Shattering all of my dreams like pieces of glass;
Self confidence asunder, hope I had none,
I had gambled on ego, and humility had won.

A LETTER TO MOTHER ON MOTHER'S DAY

Dear Mom –

This Mother's Day which I do spend
Alone with thoughts of you,
Brings back to mind the yesterdays
And the things we used to do.

I was thinking back when you were born,
Your father walked out on your mother,
When a few years later, she married again,
Bringing new sisters and brothers.

How in your fifties, I remember it well,
The trip you made with no bother,
The look of anxiousness on your face,
To see for the first time, your father.

I'm remembering too, a woman so young,
Who married and had six little girls,
And one of them died at the age of five,
So young for the sorrows of the world.

When you and papa, still so young,
Both still in your thirties, I believe,
He also died leaving you alone
To raise five little girls, including me.

It's hard to understand today,
The storms which you did weather,
I'm glad you found another to wed,
Bringing one more girl, six altogether.

We were so selfish as most kids are,
But I'm sure you understood,
That in youth, our thoughts were shallow,
But I'd change things now if I could.

I can look back now and realize,
What you did without for yourself,
How all you had were a few simple dresses,
You made yourself with what was left.

As I look back down through the years,
I can see now that I'm older,
The many things I've left undone,
I wish I'd been much bolder.

I never heard you once complain
Of things you did not possess,
But I'm sure though you must at times,
Longed for just one nice dress.

I never heard you sit and dream
Or lust for worldly things,
You were content with what God gave,
The joy which only a family brings.

As a child, of course, we never knew,
And I guess God meant it that way,
Of the sacrifices you made for us,
To show your love for us each day.

We all worked hard, no easy life,
In the fields we all did toil,
From early morn til dusky dark,
To till and work the soil.

I recall the good meals you cooked for us,
To keep our big family fed,
You knew with six little girls to raise,
We had to be thankful for our bread.

Sometimes you would go to the fields with us,
To work in the corn and cotton til night,
Come in home, prepare a good meal,
Early to bed, arise again before daylight.

We were no different from all the others,
For they too were as hard-up as we,
It was a time for all our nation
To call on the Lord, His mercy be.

I remember well, those days when young,
How you sewed the new and the worn,
So all us girls could look our best,
To go to church on Sunday morn.

You sewed new dresses for each of us,
Six girls to keep in style,
That old machine would run for weeks,
To make the right dress for each child.

Your calling always was to help,
In sickness you did go,
To lend a hand whether day or night,
To our neighbors, your love to show.

You didn't know what a vacation was,
Your job was seven days a week,
No thoughts of time away from home
For relaxation and rest to seek.

You wanted to give us everything,
As mothers do for their own,
But you gave us the best of all,
A mom and dad and a family home.

Although the days were harsh at times,
We had lots of fun anyway,
Through tears, sorrows, love and joy,
It made us what we are today.

We had good times, we laughed a lot,
We had each other to entertain,
God turned our sorrows into joy,
And graciously erased the pain.

In later years, when we were gone,
And you and dad had time alone,
You could enjoy some of the better things,
And you had a nice dress all of your own.

As I look back now, you stood far
Above all the earthly mothers,
You were my friend, I could depend
On you when I had no others

I've spent this day alone with thee,
But I am not lonely, you see,
For I, like you, have weathered the storm,
And God has been so good to me.

You see that we are older now,
Our lives will soon end too,
And we shall greet the Lord our God
In Heaven, there soon to be with you.

I know you're happy now with Christ,
It is I, with sadness, who reminisce,
But I just wanted to visit with you,
To say I love you and how I miss.

This day of honor is just about spent,
And I graciously honor thee,
I'm always glad to have the chance
To recall our lives in memory.

I must close now this letter to you,
For I can barely see,
The tears are flowing down my cheeks,
On these pages the splatters be.

My eyes are blurred with all these tears,
These words I dimly see,
I'll say goodbye now and I thank you,
For spending this Mother's Day with me.

I must arise, there are things to do,
This letter much longer than planned,
But I'm so glad for this special day,
To honor all mothers throughout the land.

Your daughter

Who can find a virtuous woman? for her price is far above rubies. Many daughters have done virtuously, but thou excellest them all. (Prov. 31:10 & 29 KJV)

WHY DO WE SUFFER?

Dear God in Heaven

Thank you for my home on earth,
Though I'm the only one in it,
All else have gone except for me,
Alone, sometimes defeated;
My sorrow sometimes overwhelms
My soul to near disaster,
If not but for my faith in thee,
My God, my Lord, my Master,
I'd be so lost, so sad and torn,
Between my grief and laughter.

My pain, dear Lord, I do endure,
With questions gone unanswered,
But sometimes, with fleeting ease,
My painless joy unhampered,
I graciously extend my thanks,
One brief relief undampered;
Some say, dear Lord, it is your plan,
Thy children sometime to suffer,
"All things work together for good,
To those who love the Lord,"
I hear so often quoted,
But mostly, though, it seems to be,
Those who are well, I've noted.

Now others say, it's not God's will,
For unhappiness, pain, or sorrow,
Or sickness, our lives to shatter;
He wants us well, prosperous, full of joy,
Our lives, he wants no sadder;

Now Lord, I've thought betwixt the two,
And so resolve the matter,
For human nature as it is,
I will, when well, believe the former,
But when I'm sick, the latter.

For God can use sorrow in our lives to help us turn away from sin and seek salvation. We will never regret that kind of sorrow. But sorrow without repentance is the kind that results in death. (II Cor. 7:10 NLT)

I WONDER

I wonder Lord so long ago
When that bright star appeared,
Did it sparkle bright with heavenly light,
Did it draw the shepherds near?
  I wonder

When they found the babe in swaddling clothes,
Did he have a special glow,
Was his face alight with glory bright,
Did the sheep and cattle low?

When the angel appeared to Mary, Lord,
Did you have thoughts of another,
How did you make your choice of her,
To be the Messiah's mother?
  I wonder

And Lord, what did Joseph think,
When told of Mary's plight,
Before God revealed to him
That everything was all right?

When they returned to Nazareth town,
On that long and dusty road,
Did the baby cry when he grew tired,
Did the donkey tire of the load?
  I wonder

As a child, dear Lord, did Jesus cry,
When he skinned his knee at play,
Did his mother hold him in her arms,
And kiss his hurt away.

And Lord, the wonder of them all,
When on the cross you died,
How could Mary bear her hurt inside,
To see you crucified?
  I wonder

How could she ever understand,
That it was planned and just,
For God to make a way to Heaven,
She had to give her son to die for us?

Now Lord, of all these wonders,
Many more left untold,
If need be, in all your wisdom,
To me you will unfold.

So I'll not fret or worry more,
Content with thee I'll be,
If ever you want to tell me though,
My ear I'll lend to thee.

In thee, O Lord, do I put my trust: let me never be put to confusion. (Ps. 71:1 KJV)

THE OLD MAN

In a run-down part of town one day,
I met this unforgettable man,
Happily whistling a merry tune,
Collecting his food from a garbage can.

I said to him, “Hello, there sir,
So happy you seem to be,
Tell me, I pray, what is the key
To all of this joy and frivolity?"

He stopped and listened, then turned my way,
And with a crinkling smile replied,
"Oh, my friend, I once was blind
But now I see, completely satisfied."

“But sir,” I said, “You have no eyes,
How then can you see?”
"Oh,” he replied, with hands held high,
"My soul has eyes within me.”

"Although no eyes my Lord provides,
I’m rich in wealth and fame,
I have a table prepared for me,
In a mansion all in my name.”

"But sir, the clothes you wear
Are tattered and torn in rags;
How can you say that you are rich,
When you gather your food in bags?”

"How can you say your home is
A castle with many rooms supplied,
And that you have a banquet hall,
And are served like a king?" I cried.

"You see, my friend, this life of mine,
Will live and never cease,
For I have been born again," he said,
"My Lord I long to please."

"You say that you will live forever,
That you shall never die,
The cemetery is full of bones," said I,
"How then can death not pass you by?"

"You too can live and never die,"
The old man said to me,
"If you will only ask the Lord,
To let your blind eyes see."

"To forgive your sins and enter in
Your life to set you free,
To live His life through you each day,
More like Him to be."

I then bade the old man goodbye,
Shaking my head and grinning;
But as I continued my journey on,
I was greatly aware of sinning.

When I returned home late that night,
A wretched soul was I;
I could not sleep and found myself
On the floor where I did lie.

And as I made my peace with God,
I asked Him please to remember,
The dear old man who changed my life,
In just one brief encounter.

I know that mansion is prepared,
For both my friend and me,
And one day soon, we'll both live there,
To spend eternity.

I knew for sure that dear old man
Has at least one reward,
For the witness that he gave to me,
To bring me to the Lord.

Those who listen to instruction will prosper; those who trust the Lord will be happy. (Prov. 16:20 NLT)

TOO BUSY

Now I'm nobody's busybody,
For I do not let my tongue wag,
I never say nothing to no one,
And my mouth, I sometimes do gag,
And if, by chance, I don't like someone
For being so haughty and proud,
I just turn up my nose and then
I say what I think aloud,
But I will not criticize anyone today,
And that's all I'm going to say.

I go to church most every Sunday
To see just who is there,
If the preacher visited the sick or not,
Or even if he cared;
He may have played golf on Thursday,
Instead of doing his job just so,
And when the girls come over for tea,
I'll just casually let them know,
But I will not criticize anyone today,
And that's all I'm going to say.

When I heard Mrs. Pickett talk
About her neighbor across the street,
I said not a word to encourage her,
For I knew she was a cheat,
And when she told how fat she was,
I said she eats too many sweets,
That she talked a way too much,
Wore shoes too small for her feet,
But I will not criticize anyone today,
And that's all I'm going to say.

When the husband of Mrs. Watson
Came in very late one night,
They said he was probably playing around,
That he really wasn't too bright,
But I never opened my mouth, you see,
Cause I knew that they were right,
And when he drank and got to full,
It was a terrible, terrible sight,
But I will not criticize anyone today,
And that's all I'm going to say.

When Mr. Rivers died last week,
'Twas really such a loss,
You know, he gambled an awful lot,
They said he was a terrible boss;
He abused his wife and children too,
And lied again and again,
'Tis a shame he died the way he did,
Was such a dear, dear man,
But I will not criticize anyone today,
And that's all I'm going to say.

I don't have time to do all I should,
For I am so busy, you know,
To visit the sick or listen to those
Who have all those sorrows and woes,
To feed the poor, I find such a bore,
No need to pray for your brothers,
But there's one thing you can say of me,
I sure don't gossip about others,
But I will not criticize anyone today,
And that's all I'm going to say.

In the multitude of words there wanteth not sin: but he that refraineth his lips is wise. (Prov. 10:19 KJV)

THE OLD ROCKING CHAIR

That old rocking chair that used to sit
In winter, before the open fire,
Was like one of our family members,
It worked hard, never seeming to tire.

It creaked and groaned beneath the load,
But never, never failed;
It was a steadfast friend of ours,
Its endurance we gladly hailed.

It rocked the babies to sleep at night,
Always with loving care,
And when you wanted just to rest,
You could always sit down there.

The rhythmic motion back and forth
Could lull you fast asleep,
It soothed your nerves at end of day,
Brought snores from way down deep.

You sat there when you were happy,
And rocked and hummed a tune;
You sat there when you were sad,
And wept bitter tears of doom.

Sometimes for no reason at all,
You found yourself embraced
By the arms of that old rocking chair,
Where loving memories graced.

At other times, it held two or three,
Just as many as could pile on;
It laughed along with all the kids,
Just glad to be a part of home.

Although it’s tired now, not much use,
It sits in the corner alone;
You just don't turn your back on a friend,
And put it out of your home.

Why, that old chair is a part of me,
It knows my grief and sorrows;
My deepest secrets it has kept,
And will share in my tomorrows.

I know the day will surely come,
For all things must have an end,
When that old chair will have to go,
And I shall lose a friend.

But in the meantime, we'll just sit
Together in no hurry,
For that old chair may outlive me,
Then I won't have to worry.

The Lord is my shepherd; I have everything I need.
(Ps. 23:1 NLT)

THE SPIDER

I sit entranced, mind's door unclosed,
In awe of nature's wonder;
This thing I see to ponder,
The deity of God exposed.

This tiny little creature so
Busily and quietly weaving,
Intricate design achieving,
Threads delicate, yet strongly flow.

Four pairs of legs, he has to build
His web up high or low;
Adding his silk to hold his web so
Wingless body can move, as willed.

His complex work like spokes of wheel,
Withstands the strains of wind;
Moving back and forth and sideways, then
Using his web, he'll snare his meal.

His work all done, he steps aside,
All set with bait,
His victim await,
Self confident and satisfied.

His victim now, been lured inside,
He quickly ties with webbing,
While life is slowly ebbing;
'Twas quite a catch, he sighs.

With sated appetite, he cuts the strand,
The remains fall through the snare;
His web he'll now repair,
Then steps aside and patiently waits again.

We can be sure, if trust we give
To Him above,
With all our love,
Our needs He will fulfill.

If God, with loving care, has given to the spider,
Wisdom and skill,
His snare to build,
How much more He'll be our provider.

The spider taketh hold with her hands, and is in kings' palaces.
(Prov. 30:28 KJV)

A DAY'S WORK

The rooster crows 'tis time to rise,
To greet the dawn through darkened skies,
He speaks to me that day has come,
And there is much that must be done.

Cows to milk and hogs to feed,
Horses to hitch to plant the seed,
Corn to plant and cotton to hoe,
And dusty swirls down each long row.

If God in mercy lets each grow tall,
We'll harvest the crop come early next fall,
So giddy-up Mert why go so slow,
We've much to do before we go.

Rows to plow while there is light,
Before the day fades into night,
And darkness comes to dim our view,
To lay its bed of moisture dew.

Miles to go this early morn,
To hoe the cotton and plant the corn,
Much to do in sunshine bright
Before our slumber in the night.

Yes, much to do while there is light,
To find sweet slumber in the night.

OUR MYSTERY MAN

There was this old man in our town,
Who lived by himself, all alone,
He had a one-room shack nestled in the trees,
Where he lived and called his home;
I never heard of his visiting anyone,
And if he had a family, I knew of none.

I remember we kids would often pass by,
And we'd stare and wonder why
This strange man lived all alone by himself,
What would happen to him, should he die;
Why, he must have been one hundred back then,
At least to us kids, he would have been.

He was tall and thin and very frail,
With an old worn hat on his head,
Of course, he would never harm a soul,
But we were curious as to the life he led;
In our little minds, we gave him a mysterious look,
To fit into our little detective book.

He would often walk a couple of miles
To the little country store to buy his food,
While we gazed and whispered to each other,
And imagined wild stories so rude;
We were little detectives trying to figure out,
Why he lived alone with no-one else about.

We were too scared to venture near,
After all, we made him what he was not,
We didn't want him to be a regular fellow,
For he had to fit into our little plot;
I can still see the smoke rising up from the stack,
While he sits outside of his one-room shack.

I never knew of him ever to work,
Or where he got his money to live on,
He had two or three old hound dogs in the yard,
Who would bark and growl when he was gone;
I wonder if his life might have been
Different, perhaps, if he'd had a friend.

But the years passed by, we kids grew up,
And our detective story came to an end,
Our mystery character was just an old man,
Who lived alone with the rain and the wind;
And the smoke from his chimney rising high in the sky,
Sent a special greeting to all who passed by.

Years later, after leaving our little home town,
We heard that the frail little man
Had gotten ill in his old age,
And a family extended a helping hand;
With kindness and mercy and a home supplied,
They cared for him till the old man died.

It's things like this in a small little town,
That happen without fame and fanfare,
It's just a part of everyday life,
To the people who care and live there;
Yes, there are still people who will do a favor,
And obey God's law and help thy neighbor.

Love worketh no ill to his neighbour: therefore love is the fulfilling of the law. (Rom. 13:10 KJV)

LOOKING THROUGH MY WINDOW

Listen now and be very still
And not even move a whit,
And act as though you're dead,
Not batting an eye as you sit,
I'll tell you something you can see,
To amuse yourself as it does me.

This little creature comes zooming in,
Yet lands on the birdbath so light,
Sometimes it's red, sometimes it's blue,
Sometimes it's brown with a little white;
That he is beautiful, I'm sure he knows,
By the way he stands in a stately pose.

His keen little eyes are always alert,
Constantly moving to and fro,
But if he catches one little move,
He'll fly away fast, away he'll go,
But if you'll just sit and wait him out,
He'll think you're a statue, no life about.

And when he's sure all things are safe,
Stepping quickly in, he feels the cool,
As the water through his feathers ooze,
Although he's in, he's nobody's fool,
He turns his head and looks again,
Right straight at you, the statue man.

All cautions gone, he ducks his head
In motions left and right,
He splashes water round about
And flitters and flutters with all his might,
Enjoying himself, he looks once more,
Did I miss something when I looked before?

It matters not about the weather,
To him it's all the same,
I've seen him bathe in winter's cold,
And splash and play a little game,
And when the snow has filled his space,
I've seen the sadness in that little face.

When his bath is done, he hops on the rim
Of the birdbath where he'll stand,
And look around as if to say,
I've had a bath and I feel grand,
With one last look, he flies away,
But he'll return another day.

For these little feathered friends of mine,
Will come back again and again,
And I will play this game with them,
For I'm their friend, the statue man,
But you cannot move or blink your eye,
For if you do, away they'll fly.

A LETTER TO DAD ON FATHER'S DAY

Dear Dad –

Although you were a step-dad to me,
You raised me from a child,
Along with five other little girls,
I know we drove you wild;
So on this special Father's Day,
I have a few little words to say.

I look back now and wonder how
You ever made the choice,
To marry a widow with five little girls,
And you had one also to voice;
But I'm so glad you had the wit,
And I hope you never regretted it.

For you see, you were so good to us,
And times back then were tough,
But God's mercy brought us through,
We can never thank Him enough;
You had to toil and work a lot,
In the winter's cold and the summer's hot.

I remember you used to worry a lot,
Before you found a new life,
But when Christ came into your heart,
The worries vanished and all the strife;
You were well past middle age by then,
But Jesus Christ forgave your sins.

I thought you were always a good man,
You were a moral man, a good dad,
But when you committed your life to Christ,
Happiness and joy erased the sad;
There was a difference, a change about,
And the goodness of God came flowing out.

I remember you once said to me,
You felt led to tithe, but how,
You just didn't have the money,
And the worry showed on your furrowed brow;
Then it seemed as though you heard God say,
Why don't you throw those cigarettes away?

That very moment you made the choice,
God's word you would obey,
You never smoked again since then,
The money for tithes was paid that day;
Yes, you followed God at his command,
You let Him lead you by the hand.

You witnessed to everyone you met,
How Jesus had saved your soul,
You testified to all who'd hear,
How they, too, could be made whole;
I thank you for the life you led,
As I recall the things you said.

Yes, the memories will always remain,
But the one that stays with me,
Is the example you set for us to follow,
Of how a Christian life should be;
For your witness you gave was not in vain,
It strengthens me daily again and again.

So I honor you this Father's Day,
Though you no longer here abide,
You now reside in Heaven
With mama by your side;
I send this letter to you with love,
We'll see you soon with Christ above.

Your daughter

Keep me from lying to myself; give me the privilege of knowing your law. I have chosen to be faithful; I have determined to live by your laws. (Ps. 119:29,30 NLT)

IN REVERIE

While looking out the window,
Just lost in silent musings,
My thoughts in random choosings
Into my head do flow;
Transfixed in all my reveries,
My empty thoughts embracing,
In solitude erasing
Those things that clutter the soul;
With vessel cleaned and emptied,
Restored and now refilling,
A fresh and new revealing
Of thoughts dispersed made whole.

Search me, O God, and know my heart: try me, and know my thoughts: And see if there be any wicked way in me, and lead me in the way everlasting. (Ps. 139:23,24 KJV)

Reflections

IN TIME

OF

PRAYER

PRAYER

Dear God in Heaven –

Forgive my sins of jealousy, greed, and pride,
And cleanse my heart and make it pure
With love and joy supplied;
And Lord God help me, my faith to grow,
Thy word to read and ponder,
And in thy grace, help me to show
My love for you more fonder.

Amen

The Lord is nigh unto them that are of a broken heart; and saveth such as be of a contrite spirit. (Ps. 34:18 KJV)

PRAYER

Dear Lord Jesus, I come to thee,
To thank you for my being,
Where blind in faith I used to be,
Opened thou mine eyes for seeing;
My heart of stone, I called my own,
Was proud and selfish giving,
Not knowing of your love and peace,
You offered for my living,

You gave me hope and life anew,
In thee I came believing,
With a little faith as a mustard seed,
Repenting and receiving;
To grow in grace, I sought thy face,
Thy word to me consoling,
Thou art my God, my Lord, my all,
Merciful and all knowing.

O Give thanks unto the Lord; call upon his name: make known his deeds among the people. (Ps. 105:1 KJV)

PRAYER

Dear God in Heaven –

With thankful hearts we come to thee,
To thank you for your blessings,
For bread we eat and clothes we wear,
Our sins to you confessing;
For those, dear God, who are in need,
Help us with compassion,
To pray and give, their needs to fill,
And point them to salvation.

Amen

O Sing unto the Lord a new song: sing unto the Lord, all the earth. (Psalm 96:1 KJV)

PRAYER

I praise you in the early morn
Upon rising from my sleep,
And ere before the day begins,
I thank you for my keep;
Before I start the day anew,
I turn again to you in prayer,
For what I know the day will bring,
Like freshness from an April shower.

The newness of a brand new day
With all its spiritual blessings,
Like gentle rain upon the flowers,
So loving and caressing;
All through the day my thoughts are versing,
Though not aloud so one can hear,
The praises to my loving Lord,
Upon my lips so very near.

I need thee in all my dealings
With friends and foes alike,
Whomever comes into my presence,
Let me reveal thy light;
When day is spent and nighttime comes,
In my quiet time alone with thee,
I rest in peace, my sins forgiven,
In the Christ who died for me.

Pray without ceasing. (I Thess. 5:17 KJV)

PRAYER

Dear Lord, I now believe
That thou art He,
The one who was to come,
Who lived and died
For all my sins,
For me was crucified;
And that today are alive,
Arisen from the grave,
To live in hearts of all believers,
To sanctify and save;
And that one day you will return
To earth to reign as King,
With praises and with thankful hearts,
To you dear Lord we'll sing.

O Give thanks unto the Lord; for he is good: because his mercy endureth for ever. (Ps. 118:1 KJV)

Reflections

WORDS

OF

WISDOM

PRIDE

Pride is our secret sin,
We deny it to our brother,
We bring it out and boast of it,
Then hide it under cover.

FORGIVE

To forgive is always worth
The effort we put in it,
Whether the giver or receiver,
It only takes a minute.

GREED

Greed is what we see in others,
So easy for us to spot;
We are so envious in seeing them
Receive the things which we have not.

HUMILITY

Humility surrounds our entire being,
We claim it near and far,
Just give us a chance to brag of it,
We'll show you how humble we really are.

SELF RIGHTEOUSNESS

Self righteous we would ne'er admit,
'Tis not right for us to be,
Yet we wear it like a hat,
For everyone to see.

SUFFERING

If God commanded us all to suffer,
Assured us everything if we would,
We'd still spend the rest of our lives,
Trying to escape it if we could.

DAILY BREAD

God gives us our daily bread,
To share with one another,
But if we selfishly keep it all,
We dishonor our precious brother.

SECOND CHANCE

God gives us a second chance,
How merciful is He,
And if we need a third one,
He'll gladly give us three.

HOLY SPIRIT

The Holy Spirit cannot be seen,
God says it's like the wind,
We can only see the results of it,
But not the beginning or end.

SELFISHNESS

Selfishness we do hate
In others when we see,
If we ourselves can benefit,
So gratified are we.

ACROSTIC

Jesus is the Son of God,
Our Savior God did send,
He never had a beginning,
Nor does He have an end.

BITTERNESS

Bitterness is like an acid,
It gradually eats away,
Like a cancer within your body,
You must act without delay.

HAPPINESS

We cannot work for happiness,
Neither can it be bought,
Why do we strive so hard then
For something all in naught.

COVET

We covet and lust for so many things
In secret, our hearts could just burst,
Why would God give it all to them,
When He knows we deserve it first.

RICHES

Riches do not satisfy,
A lesson hard to learn,
Too many sink till they drown,
For joy and contentment they yearn.

TIME

Time is one thing we all have,
To do with what we may,
We work so hard to have the chance
To idle it away.

TONGUE

What cuts like a two-edged sword,
Powerful though small it be,
One little spark can start a fire,
For all the world to see.

TITHING

Tithing is such a noble trait,
In others we admire,
But not enough for us to give,
That same trait to acquire.

Reflections

Printed in the United States
132295LV00010B/118/A

9 781594 672231